THE POOH CRAFT BOOK

THE POOH CRAFT BOOK

INSPIRED BY
WINNIE THE POOH &
THE HOUSE AT POOH CORNER

Craft ideas and drawings by
CAROL S. FRIEDRICHSEN

Methuen Children's Books · London

First published in Great Britain 1982
by Methuen Children's Books Ltd
11 New Fetter Lane, London EC4P 4EE

Craft ideas and drawings by Carol S. Friedrichsen.

Printed in Great Britain by
Butler & Tanner Ltd, Frome and London.

British Cataloguing in Publication Data

Friedrichsen, Carol S.
  The Pooh craft book.
  1. Milne, AA. Winnie-the-Pooh   2. Milne, AA.
  House at Pooh Corner   3. Handicraft—
  Juvenile literature
  I. Title
  745.5   TT160
ISBN 0-416-23200-0

For my sons, Hans and Eric,
for whom I first made the miniature animals

Contents

Introduction

This book tells how to make miniature stuffed animals and other crafts inspired by the Pooh books. Ever since childhood, I have been enchanted by the tales about Christopher Robin, Winnie-the-Pooh, Piglet, Eeyore, and all of the other animal friends. Of course, as soon as my own children were old enough to enjoy bedtime stories, I introduced them to the Pooh books. They were equally delighted with Pooh's escapades. Our favourite adventures were read and reread until the characters and the stories came to be familiar old friends.

As my children grew older, the bedtime stories were replaced with homework assignments and other reading material, but, nostalgically, every now and then, we would remember Pooh, Piglet, or Eeyore, the Woozle Hunt, Trapping a Heffalump, or an Expotition to the North Pole. How we all enjoyed the memories of our storybook friends! This shared appreciation of A. A. Milne's literary gifts and Ernest Shepard's drawings was the inspiration that led me to create, many years ago, the miniature Pooh animals as a surprise for my children. They were originally designed for and are still used as ornaments on our Christmas tree. They will always remind us of that certain realm of fantasy that can truly be only a reality in childhood.

You can make your miniature animals to use as toys or decorations, and, although this book is written primarily for young sewers, it can be used by mothers and grandmothers to make toys for children who are too young or too inexperienced to make the animals themselves. The animals will require a considerable number of hours and it is suggested that you plan to allow several days to complete each one. You might want to make the patterns and cut the pieces at one time, then do the

sewing and finishing over a period of a few days. Of if you are very patient and like to work on a project until it is completed, plan to make an animal on a day when you can devote several hours to your project.

The Felt Pictures can be made rather quickly, once you have assembled all of your material. The time required to complete your picture will depend on the size and amount of detail. The Hunny Pot requires two work sessions with a week in between to allow the clay to dry. The Snow Scene is the quickest project to complete.

Each project begins with a list of materials you will need. It is a good idea to assemble these in one place before you start to work. Don't cut the book pages in order to have patterns to pin to the felt when making the stuffed animals or felt pictures. Use tracing paper over the drawings and trace each line carefully. Then cut out your patterns from the tracing paper.

After you have finished making all of the craft projects in this book for yourself, you might like to make your favourites to use as gifts. Hopefully, this book may inspire you to try to make other animals or to create other felt pictures. You can use the same coil method, as used in making the Hunny Pot, to create containers with different shapes. Use your imagination, have fun, and happy crafting!

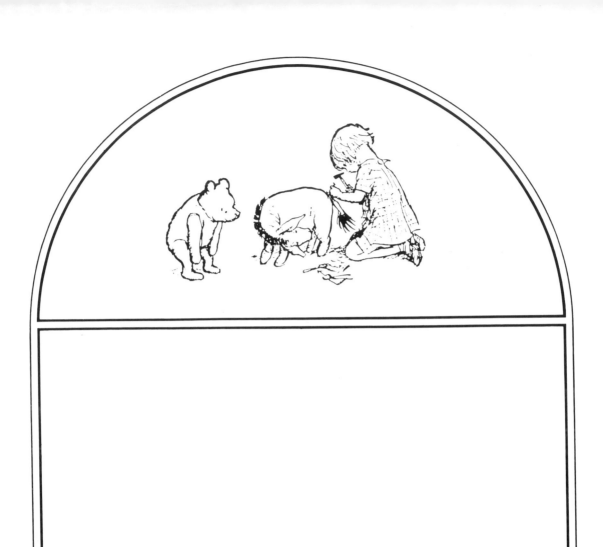

THE POOH CRAFT BOOK

"Pooh," said Rabbit kindly,
"you haven't any brain."
"I know," said Pooh humbly.
—*Winnie-the-Pooh*

PART 1

THE FELT ANIMALS

General Instructions

You will need:
tracing paper
soft lead pencil
dressmaker's pins
felt fabric, in appropriate colours
small, sharp scissors
small plastic bags
a thimble, if you sew with one
assorted sewing needles
sewing threads to match the felt
stranded embroidery cotton, in appropriate
   colours
acrylic fibre *or* kapok for stuffing
a stuffing poker—small paintbrush handle, thin
   dowel, *or* blunt pencil
shoe box *or* basket, to store your materials in

Before you begin to work, read these General Instructions completely. Then read the instructions for the individual animal that you want to make. The results will depend on how carefully and exactly you follow the patterns and the instructions. As you work, read and follow each step precisely. If you should make a mistake in constructing your animal, carefully remove the stitches and begin again. Always be sure that your hands are clean before you begin to work. The fabric will easily

become soiled if it is handled with dirty fingers.

Begin by tracing the patterns very accurately, using a soft lead pencil, and tracing paper, secured with paper clips. Take your time cutting the patterns out of the tracing paper so that you are sure to cut exactly on the line. The animals are designed to be made of felt which can be purchased in craft shops and department stores in a wide range of colours. It is usually available in 23 cm squares.

Each pattern piece should be cut from a single thickness of felt. Use small, sharp scissors, such as embroidery scissors. The patterns should be pinned to the felt using the dressmaking pins. Cut out the large pieces first, pinning the patterns near the edge of the fabric. Place each pattern piece near to the previous one cut to save on the amount of material you use. Do not cut more than one thickness at a time. If you do, you may distort the shapes and this would prevent the accurate joining of the seams and parts. When you have cut out all of the parts and pieces, put them in a small plastic bag. This will keep the tiny pieces in one place and it will keep your fabric clean.

Before you begin to sew your animal, it would be wise to practice sewing on some of the felt scraps. Cut two pieces of felt to use for your practice sewing. The pieces can be any shape. Next cut a piece of thread of the same colour as the felt (or as close a match as possible) about 1 metre long and thread it through the eye of a thin, medium-size needle. Bring the ends of the thread together and tie them in a knot. Clip off any extra thread that may extend beyond the knot. Place one piece of fabric on top of the other, and pin or hold together the edges of the two pieces to be joined. Be careful to match these edges exactly. Sew all the seams with small, overcast stitches, working from right to left. The stitches should be very tiny, about 2 mm apart and 2 mm deep. They should be worked as shown

in Figure 1. Be sure to stitch through both thicknesses of the felt. Do not pull the stitches too tightly because this will cause the felt to tear. When you reach the end of a seam or run out of thread, secure the end by taking several stitches in the same place before cutting the thread.

Figure 1.
Overcast Stitch

As you sew, you may find that the pieces you have cut do not match exactly. If this occurs, you should ease the pieces in place by taking up slightly more fabric in your stitches along the longer edge. After you have practised your stitches, sew your animal together according to the individual instructions that appear on the patterns. Use the letters, which appear as (A), (B), etc., as a guide when joining the parts. As you sew each animal, leave a small opening of 2–3 cm for stuffing.

Acrylic fibre or kapok for stuffing can be purchased in craft shops and department stores. Use tiny wisps of the stuffing material to fill the animal. Gently push the stuffing in place with your stuffing poker. Start by filling the legs until they are firm. Next, fill the head, the neck, and the body. It is important that you take time and care to do a thorough job of stuffing, as this will greatly affect the appearance of the animal. The animal should be firm but not hard. When your animal is completely stuffed, close the opening in the seam with overcast stitches.

The ears should be formed as directed in the individual instructions. Attach the ears with tiny stitches in the stitch line indicated.

Before you begin to sew the features, lightly draw them on the animal's face. Follow the pattern for the positioning of the eyes, nose and mouth.

Figure 2.
Satin Stitch

The features are embroidered in satin stitch using two strands of six-strand embroidery cotton of the right colour and a thin embroidery needle. Use a thread about 60 cm long. Do not cut too long a thread as it will tend to become tangled and

knotted. After threading the needle, make a small knot at one end of the thread. Satin stitch is similar to the overcast stitch. The stitches are made very close together to completely cover the fabric (Figure 2).

Figure 3.

If the eyes are more than one colour, embroider the eye background first, next embroider the iris, and then embroider the pupil of the eye. To sew the nose, stitch through the head from one side of the nose to the other, then over the tip (Figure 3). Do this several times until the area of the nose, as shown on the pattern, is completely covered with stitches. To make the mouth, sew through the head from one corner of the mouth to the other with one long stitch, then over the mouth line and into the corner again with another long stitch. Do this three times, always making your stitches in the same place. Then sew tiny satin stitches over the thread line that marks the mouth and through the felt (Figure 4).

Figure 4.
Tiny Satin Stitches

See the individual instructions for making and finishing each animal. Remember to take your time, and work very carefully and accurately. Your first efforts may not be perfect, especially if this is your first attempt at sewing. However, don't be discouraged, because as you sew your skill will improve. The most important thing is that you will have created your very own animal friend to play with and to love.

For the more experienced or advanced sewer who would like to make a larger version of the animals, it is suggested that you take your book to a specialist photocopying shop to have the patterns enlarged. The patterns may become slightly distorted in the process. If this should occur, you will have to alter them where necessary.

Figure 5.
Outline Stitch

The larger animals, with the exception of Owl, should be made of a fabric other than felt, such as cotton or a cotton/

polyester-blend, or a low pile, fake fur fabric.

These materials will require a different type of seam. When cutting the fabric, you should add an extra 5 mm for the seam allowance around each pattern piece. Match the pieces with the right sides of the fabric together. Pin the edges together to hold them in place and tack the seams. Then machine stitch or sew by hand with tiny running stitches or back stitches. Be sure to leave openings for turning to the right side and stuffing. To prevent the seams from pulling or puckering, make 3 mm clips into the seam allowance about every 1 cm and at every sharp curve. Be careful not to clip the seam. Turn the animal right side out and stuff, then close the seam with slip stitch.

Finish the animals according to the general and individual instructions, with the following suggestions:

1. The ears should be made of a double thickness of fabric; the lining can be of felt.

2. The features can be cut from felt of appropriate colours and appliquéd in place.

3. When joining Piglet's arms or Pooh's arms and legs, use a heavyweight thread, such as button thread. On the outside of the limbs, sew through the shank of a small button. This will ease the strain on the fabric and prevent the stitches from pulling through.

4. When making Eeyore's mane and tail, cut the yarn in appropriate lengths.

When Pooh saw what it was, he nearly fell down, he was so pleased. It was a Special Pencil Case. There were pencils in it marked "B" for Bear, and pencils marked "HB" for Helping Bear, and pencils marked "BB" for Brave Bear. There was a knife for sharpening the pencils, and india-rubber for rubbing out anything which you had spelt wrong.... And all these lovely things were in little pockets of their own in a Special Case which shut with a click when you clicked it. And they were all for Pooh.

—Winnie-the-Pooh

Rabbit

You will need:
Rabbit tan felt
white felt
tan and white sewing threads
black and white embroidery cotton
a small cotton wool ball
acrylic fibre *or* kapok

Follow the General Instructions and Figure 6 (the pattern) to cut Rabbit's body, face, and ears from the tan felt. Cut Rabbit's tummy from the white felt.

Sew the two tummy sections together along the inner seam, (D) to (C). This seam will be on the inside of the body.

Stitch one side of the face to one body section, beginning at (A) and sewing around the head to (B). Then sew the other side of the face to the other body section. Sew Rabbit's nose together from (A) to (D). Stitch both sides of the tummy sections to the body sections from (D) to (C). This will form Rabbit's legs. Join the back seam of the body from (C) towards (B), leaving an opening for stuffing. Stuff Rabbit and close the back seam according to the General Instructions.

Bring together points (E) and (F) on each ear to form a fold. With the edges of the ear facing forward, match ear points (E)

to points (E) on either side of Rabbit's head. Sew the ears in place by stitching back and forth through the head.

Follow the General Instructions to embroider Rabbit's features as shown in Figure 6. The nose and mouth are black. The eyes are white with black pupils.

Make Rabbit's whiskers by taking a tiny stitch in the felt with a single strand of white sewing thread at the places indicated on the pattern. Allow both ends of the thread to extend from the stitch. Tie these threads together over the stitch to form a knot to secure the whiskers. Then cut off the threads at about 2 cm from the stitch.

For Rabbit's tail sew the small round cotton wool ball just above (C).

"Hallo, Rabbit, isn't that you?"

"No," said Rabbit.

"But isn't that Rabbit's voice?"

"I don't *think* so," said Rabbit. "It isn't *meant* to be."

"Oh!" said Pooh.

He took his head out of the hole, and had another think, and then he put it back, and said:

'Well, could you very kindly tell me where Rabbit is?"

"He has gone to see his friend Pooh Bear, who is a great friend of his."

"But this *is* Me!" said Bear, very much surprised.

"What sort of Me?"

"Pooh Bear."   —*Winnie-the-Pooh*

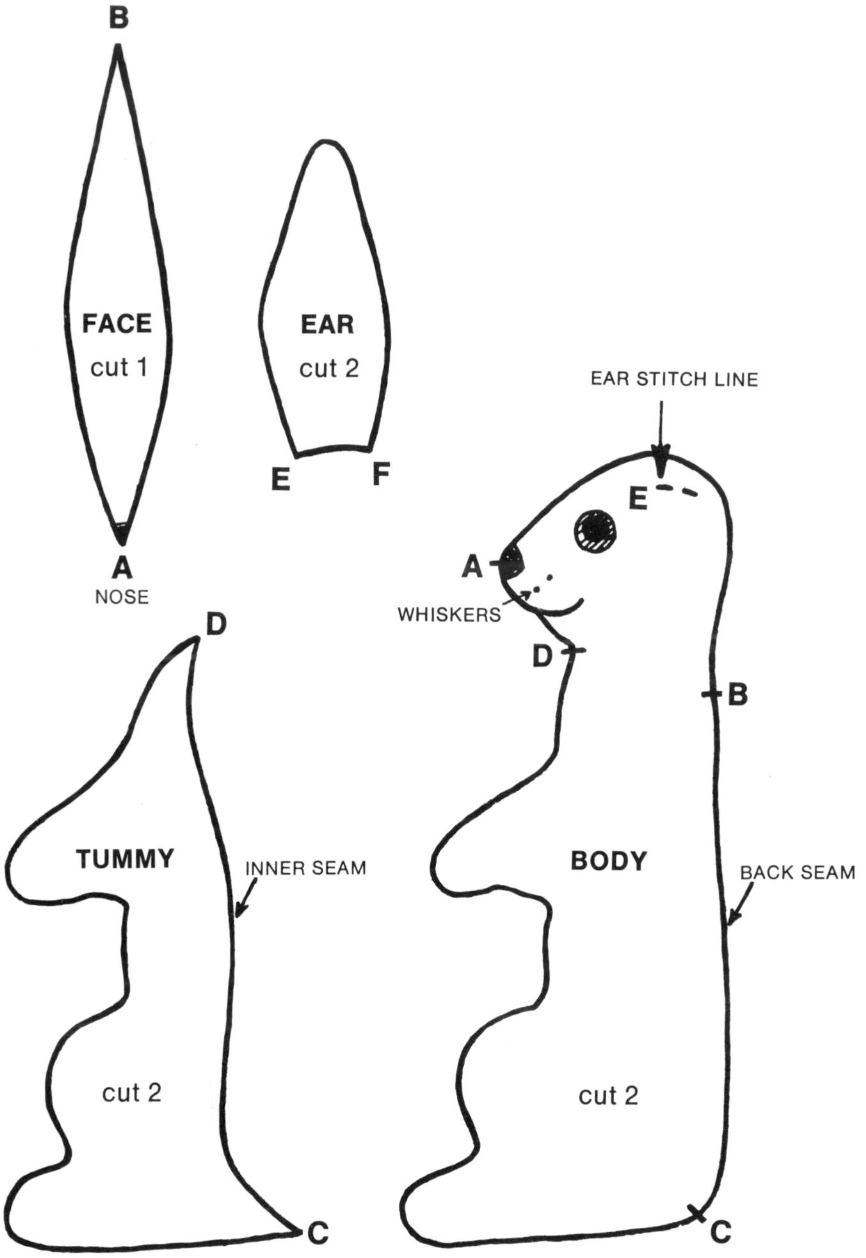

B

FACE

cut 1

A

NOSE

EAR

cut 2

E   F

EAR STITCH LINE

E

A

WHISKERS

D

D   B

TUMMY

INNER SEAM

BODY

BACK SEAM

cut 2

cut 2

C   C

Figure 6. Rabbit

Eeyore

You will need:
Eeyore grey felt
grey and black sewing threads
black 4-ply knitting-yarn
black and white embroidery cotton
small (about 5 mm) black *or* grey button with
   shank at back
acrylic fibre *or* kapok

Follow the General Instructions and Figure 7 (the pattern) to cut all Eeyore's part from the grey felt.

Stitch one side of the face section at forehead (A) to one body section (A). Continue sewing around Eeyore's nose to (B). Then sew the other side of the face to the other body section.

Stitch the tummy sections together from (C) to (D) on the inner seam only, not the legs. This seam will be towards the inside of the body. Sew the tummy sections to the sides of the body, one side at a time, stitching around the legs from (C) to (D). Sew the back seam together from (D) towards (A), leaving an opening for stuffing.

Stuff Eeyore and close the back seam according to the General Instructions.

On each ear, bring points (E) together and stitch. Attach the

ears at (X EARS) with points (E) towards the head.

Cut 22 to 24 4-cm strands of the black yarn for Eeyore's mane and forelock. Lay a strand horizontally across the neck seam beginning at the forehead and stitch it in place using a black, double sewing thread and the overcast stitch (Figure 1).

Continue in this manner, attaching each strand, one after the other, until all of the strands are in place along Eeyore's neck.

Following the General Instructions, embroider the features in the positions shown in Figure 7. The eyes have a white background with black pupils. The nostrils and the mouth are black.

Next cut four pieces of black yarn 4 to 5 cm long. Fold them in half and stitch them in place at the tip of Eeyore's tail. Bring the sides of the tail, at (F), together over the yarn and continue to stitch along the edge of the tail to the top. Flatten out the tail so that the seam will be centred under the tail when it is attached to the body. Sew the tail to the body at (X TAIL). Now sew the button on top of the tail where you have joined it to the body. The button will look like the head of the nail which Christopher Robin used to fix Eeyore's tail in its right place again.

Now that you have attached Eeyore's tail, he is ready for frisking about.

The Old Grey Donkey, Eeyore, stood by himself in a thistly corner of the Forest, his front feet well apart, his head on one side, and thought about things. Sometimes he thought sadly to himself, "Why?" and sometimes he thought, "Wherefore?" and sometimes he thought, "Inasmuch as which?"—and sometimes he didn't quite know what he *was* thinking about.   —*Winnie-the-Pooh*

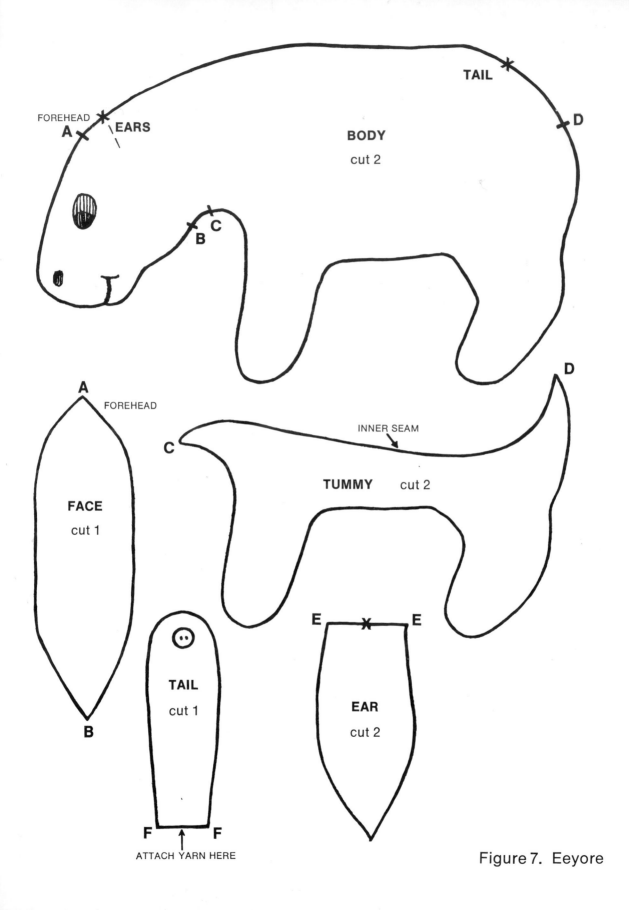

Figure 7. Eeyore

Winnie-the-Pooh

You will need:
Pooh gold felt
red felt
gold and red sewing threads
a small (about 5 mm), white button
black embroidery cotton
acrylic fibre *or* kapok

Follow the General Instructions and Figure 8 (the pattern) to cut the required number of parts and pieces for Pooh from the gold felt. The jacket will be cut from the red felt.

Before stitching the face-back-tummy section to the body, pin together the edges of one body section and the face-back-tummy section, and then the other, taking care to accurately match (A), (B), (C), and (D). It is necessary to pin *both* body sections to the face-back-tummy section before beginning to stitch these pieces together. This will prevent distortion of the body during stitching.

Start stitching at nose point (A), around one side of the head to (B). Easing the back and tummy section in place, continue to stitch down the back to (C) and around the tummy to (D). Stitch the other side of Pooh's body the same way. Be sure to leave an opening in the tummy for the stuffing. Stitch Pooh's face from (D) to (A).

As you sew the body, the arms, and the legs, stuff and finish them according to the General Instructions.

Use two pieces put together for each arm. Begin stitching the arms at the shoulder. Remember to leave a small opening for stuffing.

Stitch the legs, using two pieces for each one. Leave the leg open along the straight edge from (E) to (F). Next add each foot section to each leg by stitching from (E) to (F), leaving one side open for stuffing.

Attach Pooh's ears by stitching them in place along the ear stitch line, as shown in Figure 8, matching points (K) and (L).

Follow the General Instructions to embroider Pooh's features in the positions shown in Figure 8. Pooh's eyes, his eyebrows, nose and mouth are black.

Now you are ready to attach Pooh's arms and legs at the appropriate X's on his body. The arms and the legs will be movable if you are sure to attach them as follows. Use a large, sharp, threaded needle to stitch through the body from (X-A) to (X-A). Next stitch through one arm from (X-A) to (X-A). Now stitch back through the arm and the body in almost the same place. Add the other arm in the same manner, and stitch back and forth through the body and limbs several times for a strong joint, always being sure to follow the previous stitches. Tie off the thread around the stitches between one arm and the body.

Attach Pooh's legs at (X-L) using the same method described for attaching Pooh's arms.

Cut Pooh's jacket out of the red felt. Fold the jacket at the shoulders. Sew the seams together from (G) to (H) and from

(I) to (J). Sew the button in the position shown on the right jacket front. Cut a corresponding buttonhole as shown on the left jacket front. Slip the jacket on Pooh and button it up.

Now your Pooh is ready for adventures in the 100 Aker Wood or your very own favourite adventuring place.

"You're the Best Bear in All the World."
—*Winnie-the-Pooh*

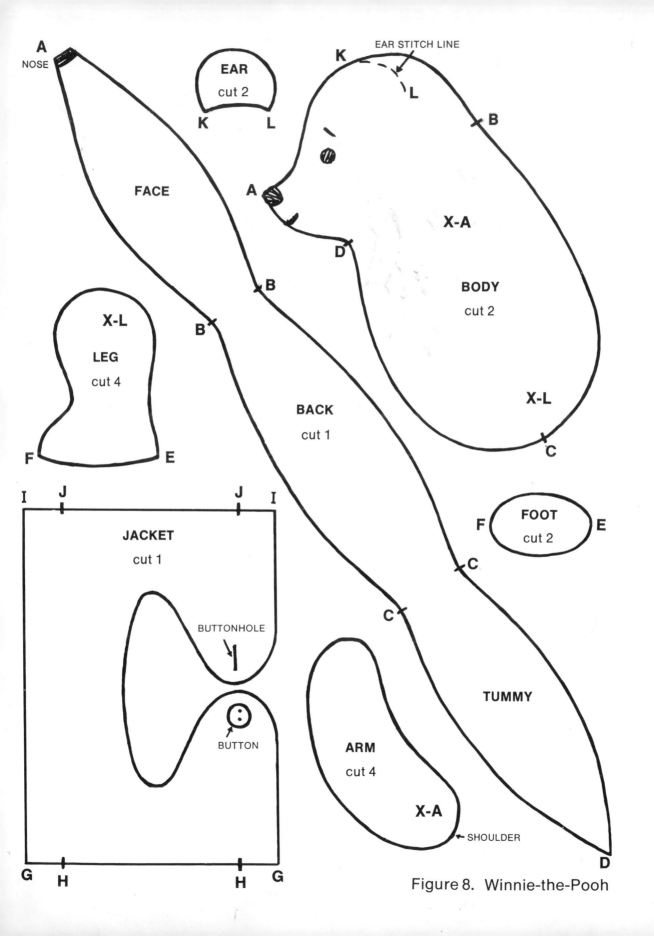

Figure 8. Winnie-the-Pooh

Kanga and Roo

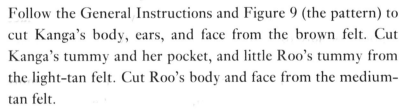

You will need:
Kanga brown felt
light–tan felt
medium–tan felt
brown and tan sewing threads
brown, black, and white embroidery cotton
acrylic fibre *or* kapok

Follow the General Instructions and Figure 9 (the pattern) to cut Kanga's body, ears, and face from the brown felt. Cut Kanga's tummy and her pocket, and little Roo's tummy from the light-tan felt. Cut Roo's body and face from the medium-tan felt.

Make Kanga first. Sew one side of the face section to the body section beginning at nose points (A) and continuing around the head to (B). Attach the face to the other body piece in the same manner. Sew the nose seam from (A) to (C).

Sew the tummy sections together along the inner seam from (C) to (D). This seam will be on the inside of the body. Stitch the tummy sections to the body sections from (C) to (D), thereby forming Kanga's legs.

Sew the back seam together from (B), around the tail towards (D), leaving an opening for stuffing. Stuff Kanga and close the seam according to the General Instructions.

Stitch Kanga's pocket in place by carefully matching pocket points (E) with body points (E). Follow the pocket stitch line shown in Figure 9 and ease the pocket slightly to fit in place.

Stitch Kanga's ears to both sides of her head on the ear stitch line shown in Figure 9, matching points (J) and (K).

Follow the General Instructions to embroider Kanga's features in the positions shown on the pattern. Kanga's nose and mouth are black. The background of the eyes is white. The iris is brown with a black pupil. There is a brown line embroidered across the eye background just above the iris. It is this line that gives Kanga's eyes their gentle, affectionate, motherly expression. Use the outline stitch (Figure 5) to make this line.

Now sew baby Roo together. Starting at points (F) of the face and one body section, stitch one side of the face and body around to (G). Now stitch the other body section to the face section. Be sure to allow the tiny ears to extend above the face piece.

Stitch the tummy sections together along the inner tummy seam from (H) to (I). This seam will be on the inside of the body. Sew the tummy sections to the body sections, from (H) to (I), thus forming Roo's legs.

Stitch the body together from (I) around Roo's tail towards (G), leaving a 1-cm opening for stuffing. Stuff Roo and close the seam according to the General Instructions.

Embroider Roo's two little brown eyes in the place shown on the pattern.

Roo can now be tucked safely into Kanga's pocket.

Nobody seemed to know where they came from, but there they were in the
Forest: Kanga and Baby Roo.   —*Winnie-the-Pooh*

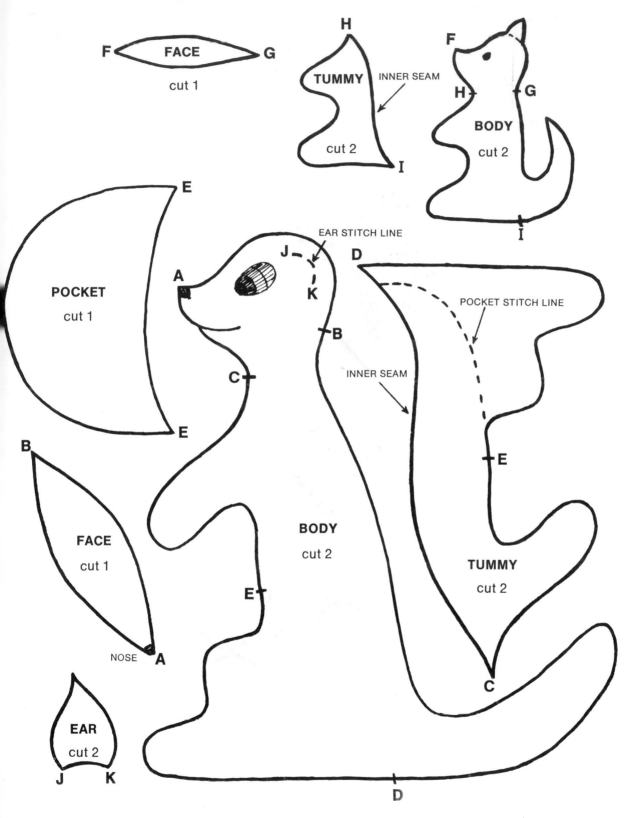

FACE cut 1

TUMMY cut 2

INNER SEAM

BODY cut 2

POCKET cut 1

EAR STITCH LINE

POCKET STITCH LINE

INNER SEAM

BODY cut 2

FACE cut 1

NOSE

TUMMY cut 2

EAR cut 2

Figure 9. Kanga and Roo

Tigger

You will need:
Tigger gold felt
gold sewing thread
black, white, and green embroidery cotton
black, waterproof, smearproof, marking pen
acrylic fibre *or* kapok

Follow the General Instructions and Figure 10 (the pattern) to cut the required pieces of Tigger from the gold felt.

Begin sewing Tigger by stitching the face to one section of the body at nose (A) and continuing around the head to (B). Sew the other body section to the face in the same manner.

Sew the tummy sections together along the inner seam from (C) to (D). This seam will be on the inside of the body. Sew nose seam from (A) to (C). Attach the tummy sections to the body sections one side at a time, stitching from (C) to (D) on each side. This forms Tigger's legs.

Sew body seam from (D), around Tigger's tail, towards (B), leaving an opening in the back seam to allow for stuffing. Stuff Tigger and close the seam according to the General Instructions.

Stitch Tigger's ears in place on the ear stitch line shown in Figure 10, matching points (E) and (F).

Follow the General Instructions and the positions shown in Figure 10 to embroider Tigger's features. His nostrils and mouth are black. Tigger's eyes have a white background with green pupils.

The body is now ready to be striped with Tigger markings. Using the marking pen follow the markings as shown in Figure 10. Be very careful to allow sufficient time for the ink to dry so that you do not smudge and smear the lines as you handle Tigger.

When Pooh awoke in the morning, the first thing he saw was Tigger, sitting in front of the glass and looking at himself.

"Hallo!" said Pooh.

"Hallo!" said Tigger. "I've found somebody just like me. I thought I was the only one of them."   —*The House at Pooh Corner*

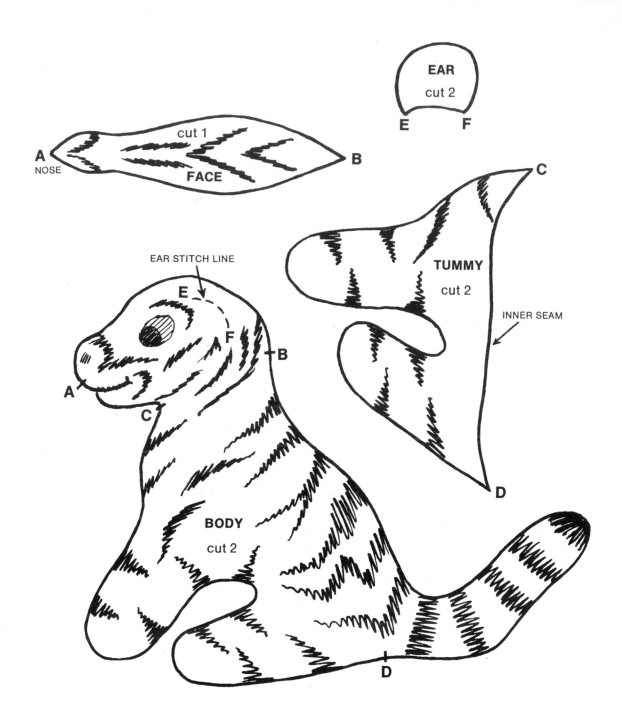

Figure 10. Tigger

Piglet

You will need:
Piglet pink felt
pink sewing thread
a 6 cm × 10 cm-piece of thin knit fabric, cotton *or*
    synthetic
pink and black embroidery cotton
acrylic fibre *or* kapok

Follow the General Instructions and Figure 11 (the pattern) to cut the required number of parts and pieces for Piglet from the pink felt.

Carefully match and hold nose point (A) on Piglet's face to nose point (A) on one side of Piglet's head. Sew the two sections together from nose point (A) around the head to (B), guiding the face section in place as you stitch. Attach the back section to the body at (C) and stitch to (D). Sew the other section of Piglet's body to the face and back sections in the same way.

Sew the head seam together from (A) to (E). Now sew the tummy to the body sections, one side at a time, from (E) to (F). Be sure to leave a small opening for stuffing near the centre of one seam. Set the body aside.

Sew the leg sections together along the straight edge from (G) to (J). This seam will be towards the inside of the body.

Now attach the leg sections to the body by sewing the leg sections to the body sections from heel points (I) to back point (J) to heel points (I). Then stitch from toe points (H) to tummy point (G) to toe points (H), thereby forming the seat and inner legs.

Stuff Piglet's body and close the tummy seam according to the General Instructions. Stuff his legs through the openings at his feet.

Sew the foot sections in place matching toe points (H) and heel points (I). As you join the foot sections, add more stuffing to the feet, if necessary, before you close the seam. The feet should not be stuffed too fully. They should be rather flat on the bottom.

Use two arm sections for each arm. Sew the pieces together beginning at the shoulders (X). Leave a small opening on one side for stuffing. Stuff the arms, then close the seams and set them aside. They will be attached later.

Now you are ready to make Piglet's suit of knit fabric (the top of a thin sock will be fine). The fabric can be in a plain colour or striped. Cut out the suit following Figure 11. Fold together the right side of the fabric as shown. Use a running stitch (Figure 12) to sew a 5 mm seam along the short side to form a tube. Turn the suit right side out. Sew a line of running stitches 5 mm from one edge but do not tie off the thread. Place the suit over Piglet's body. The suit's seam should be centred down his back. As you draw up the stitches tightly around Piglet's neck, fold the raw edge to the inside along the stitch line. Tie off the thread. Sew another row of running stitches 5 mm from the bottom edge. Turn the raw edge to the inside as you draw up the stitches to fit around the legs. Allow enough slack in the fabric and thread to stitch the bottom edge of the suit together between Piglet's legs. Tie off the thread.

¼″ SEAM

WRONG SIDE
OF FABRIC

RUNNING STITCH

Figure 12.
Piglet's Suit

The next step is to attach Piglet's arms. They will be movable if you are careful to follow these directions exactly. Use a long, sharp, threaded needle to stitch through the body from (X) to (X). Next stitch through an arm from (X) to (X). Now stitch back through the arm and the body very close to the other stitches. Attach the other arm in the same way. Stitch back and forth several times for a strong joint, always being sure to follow the previous stitches. Tie off the thread around the stitches between one arm and the body.

Sew Piglet's ears to his head at the ear stitch line shown in Figure 11, matching points (K) and (L).

Embroider Piglet's two little black eyes and his little pink nose as shown in Figure 11. Follow the embroidery directions that are explained in the General Instructions.

Now your Piglet is ready to go Woozle Hunting, join in an Expotition to the North Pole, or, best of all, he can share an exciting adventure with you.

"About as big as Piglet . . . my favourite size."
—*Winnie-the-Pooh*

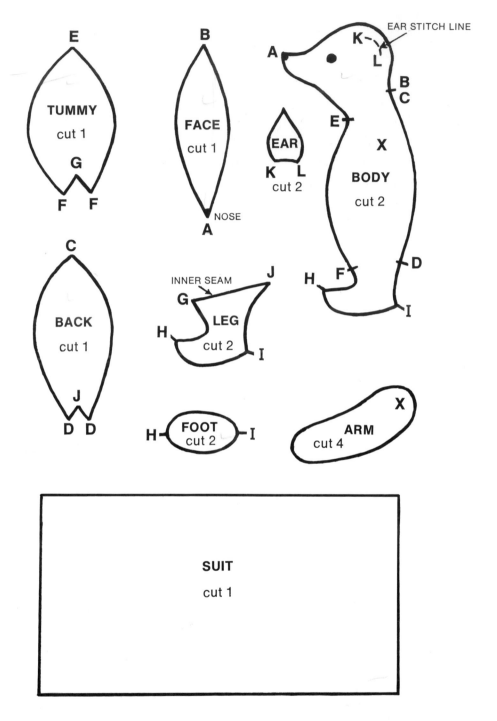

Figure 11. Piglet

Owl

You will need:
light-brown felt
medium-brown felt
grey felt
white felt
gold felt
light-brown and gold sewing threads
gold, grey, and black embroidery cotton
acrylic fibre *or* kapok
a 3 cm × 6 cm piece of thin cardboard
white fabric glue

Follow the General Instructions and Figure 13 (the pattern) to cut Owl's body, back, and wings from the light-brown felt. Cut the inner wings and tail from the grey felt, and the outer wings and large eye circles from the medium-brown felt. Owl's feathers are formed by clipping the lines as shown on four pieces in Figure 13. Cut the small eye circles from the white felt. Set aside the foot pattern.

To prepare for making Owl's feet, stick the pieces of gold felt to both sides of the thin cardboard (a piece from a cereal box would do) with fabric glue, such as Copydex. Set aside the felt-covered cardboard to dry while you make Owl's body.

First, stitch the tail under the back at points (B), allowing

the back tail feathers to overlap the tail.

Sew the back to one section of the body beginning at (A) and continuing around to (C). Attach the other body section in the same manner.

Sew the front seam together from (A) to (C), leaving an opening for stuffing. A small gap will form in the back at (C). Close this gap with a few stitches through the body and back sections. Stuff Owl, and then close the seam according to the General Instructions.

Sew the small, white eye circles in place in the centre of the large, medium-brown eye circles. Stitch the centre of the eye circles in place on Owl's face as shown in the photograph. The edges of the large circles should meet at the centre of his face. Follow the General Instructions to embroider Owl's eyes, shown on the pattern of the small eye circle. The eye background is grey, and the pupil black. Frame the eye with the outline stitch (Figure 5 on p. 17), using the black embroidery cotton. Make the beak by stitching together the edges of the large circles where they meet at the centre of Owl's face. Now satin stitch over these stitches with the gold embroidery cotton to form the beak.

Assemble the wings by placing one inner wing section under a wing and one outer wing section over the wing, matching points (D) and points (F). Stitch these three wing pieces together from (D) to (F) along the curve. Make the other wing the same way, but reverse the sections to be sure to make a right and a left wing. Now you are ready to attach Owl's wings to his body. With the wing curves towards the front of the body and the feathers towards the centre of the back, attach the wings on the stitch line shown in Figure 13. Stitch the wings to the body from (D) to (E).

The last step is to make and attach Owl's feet. Cut out two

feet (first a right, then reverse the pattern for a left) from the felt-covered cardboard pieces. Using gold thread, fasten them to the body in the place shown. Sew an X over the bottom of the foot and then make a stitch over the back claw, through the body, and between the front claws. The feet will be pliable so you can make Owl stand by bending and adjusting his claws.

If you would like Owl to appear to be flying, gently pull his wings out at the sides and push downward on the feathers that are close to his body. You can suspend him in the air by sewing a long thread through his back between his wings and hanging the thread from the ceiling or some other high place.

"Correct me if I am wrong," Owl said, "but am I right in supposing that it is a very Blusterous day outside?"
— *The House at Pooh Corner*

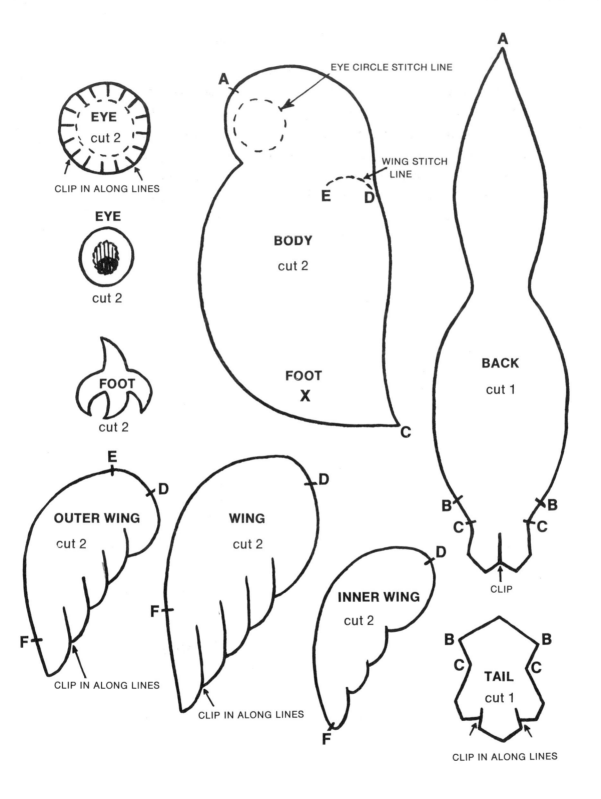

Figure 13. Owl

"It just shows what can be done by
taking a little trouble," said Eeyore.
"Brains first and then Hard Work."
—*The House at Pooh Corner*

PART 2

THREE OTHER CRAFT IDEAS

Felt Pictures

You will need:
picture frames, about 13 cm × 18 cm to 20 cm × 30 cm
thin cardboard, to fit size of frame
felt, any colour, cut to fit cardboard
felt in colours appropriate for animals, leaves, etc.
small, sharp scissors
dressmaker's pins
white fabric glue
a black, waterproof, smearproof, marking pen
tracing paper
a soft lead pencil *or* felt-tipped pen
assorted trimmings

Prepare the background for your picture by gluing the piece of felt you've chosen to the cardboard with fabric glue such as Copydex. Set the background aside to dry while you prepare the other parts of the picture.

Using tracing paper, trace one of the pictures provided (Figures 14, 15, 16) with a soft lead pencil, or choose an illustration from one of the Pooh books and draw freehand, whatever characters you would like. This drawing will be your pattern. The size of your drawing should be determined by the size of the frame that you have chosen. Colourful, plastic frames are ideal. You will not need the glass that comes with

most frames. If the frame is small, make your drawing small enough to fit inside the frame but do not make it too small. If your frame is large, make the drawing large enough to fill most of the area so that Pooh, Piglet, or Eeyore does not look lost.

Carefully cut out your patterns from the tracing paper. You can make each animal in one piece or you can make the body, head, legs, and ears separately. Pin the patterns to the felt, then cut out the pieces accurately along the edges of the patterns.

The glue on the background will now be dry. Trim away any extra fabric that might extend beyond the edge of the cardboard. When you have done this, place the background in the frame. The felt side should be in the front of the frame.

You are now ready to arrange your animal or animals on the felt background. When you have arranged the pieces in the desired positions and when you are satisfied with the appearance of your picture, carefully lift one piece at a time, apply the glue, and stick it in its proper position. Do this until all of the pieces have been attached to the picture. When the glue is dry, add lines with the black marking pen to show a joint or seam in the body, features on a face, or details in the background. Add the trimmings to the picture: a small button for Pooh's jacket, black yarn or fringe for Eeyore's mane and tail, black beads for Piglet's eyes, and any other items you think of that will add dimension and give your picture a realistic appearance.

You may want to include plants or leaves in your picture. The leaves can be cut individually from green felt. Try to place them on the picture as they would hang from a tree or grow up from the earth. Felt is very pliable and can be shaped to resemble real leaves. You can achieve a realistic effect by not gluing them down completely. To hold the leaves in place, use a small amount of glue on the edge or tip of the leaf where it

will be fastened to the background.

The animals will have a rounded appearance if you add a small amount of acrylic fibre or kapok between their bodies and the background. Be sure to apply a line of glue around the entire edge of the body before securing it in place on the background with pins until the glue dries. This is a rather difficult procedure and it would not be recommended for your first picture.

Your picture can be very simple, or it can be very detailed. You will find many other trimming materials that you can use to give your picture its own individual appearance. You are limited only by your imagination.

They came round the corner, and there was Eeyore's house, looking as comfy as anything.

"There you are," said Piglet.

"Inside as well as outside," said Pooh proudly.

Eeyore went inside . . . and came out again.

"It's a remarkable thing," he said. "It *is* my house, and I built it where I said I did, so the wind must have blown it here. And the wind blew it right over the wood, and blew it down here, and here it is as good as ever. In fact, better in places."   — *The House at Pooh Corner*

Figure 14.

TOP

Figure 15.

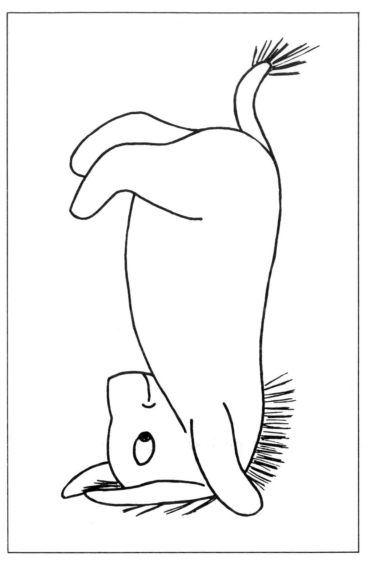

Figure 16.

Hunny Pot
(A Useful Jar to Keep Things In)

You will need:
a 45 cm square of oilcloth or thick polythene
    suitable for finishing without firing clay
a rolling pin
an old table knife
a ruler
thick cardboard
a small bowl of water
an old newspaper
a small paintbrush
acrylic artist's colour or poster paints

If you choose a product such as Newclay, which comes in 5-kilo packages, you will have a lot of clay. Perhaps you, or you and a group of friends, can plan to make several pots. You will have enough clay for ten or twelve. You should make and dry all of the pots first, then plan to decorate them later.

Since the clay will stick to most surfaces, a piece of oilcloth or polythene, 45 cm square, should be used to prevent it from sticking to your work area. Sprinkle a few drops of water on your work surface and place the oilcloth, with the shiny side down or the piece of polythene, on the wet spot. Smooth it out flat. This will prevent it from slipping around too much as you work the clay.

If you are using Newclay you will find that it is ready to be worked when you open the wrapping. If you are using a different clay follow the directions on the package to prepare it. Pinch off a piece about the size of a small egg. Roll the clay into a ball shape between the palms of your hands; then pat it until it is round and flat like a pancake. Place the pat of clay on the centre of the oilcloth and roll it flat with the rolling pin until it is about 5 mm thick and 80 mm in diameter. If the round shape becomes distorted, you should trim away the extra clay with the table knife to make it round again. This will be the bottom of your pot, the jar base. Set the base aside on a 20 cm square of cardboard.

Now pinch off another piece of clay about half the size of the first. Roll this piece between your palms to form a long cylinder. Place it on the oilcloth and continue to roll it with your palms and fingers. Work from the middle towards the ends to draw the cylinder out into a long coil about the thickness of a pencil. The coil should be long enough to go completely around the edge of the jar base. With a small paintbrush, or your finger, apply some water to the top edge of the jar base. Place the coil on top of the jar base until it completely encircles the top edge (Figure 17). Cut the ends at a slight angle, then moisten the cut with water and seal the joint. Press the coil firmly in place. Be sure that there are no open spaces between the coil and the base.

Figure 17.

Make another coil in the same way. Paint the top of the first coil with water. Place the second coil on top of the first coil, but do not join the ends over the joint of the first coil. In order to make your pot stronger, the joints should always be in a different place. Press the second coil firmly in position on top of the first. Smooth out any cracks with a little water applied with your fingertips. Continue to work in this manner, keeping the sides of your jar straight and the circumference round, until the pot is about 8 cm high.

Now you are ready to form the neck of your jar. Make two more coils. Place the first one towards the inside edge of the previous coil. Do the same thing with the next one. This will make the neck of your jar a little smaller than the body.

To form the lip of the jar, roll another coil slightly fatter than the others. Place it towards the outside, on top of the last coil (Figure 18). Now carefully look over your pot to be sure that all of the seams and joints are completely sealed. Smooth any cracks or rough places with your fingertips and a very little water. Do not use too much water or the clay will become soft and your pot might collapse. If there are any large cracks, they can be filled with small pieces of clay and water.

Let your pot dry for a few hours, then turn it upside down. Using a pencil and being very careful not to press too heavily, sign the bottom of the pot with your initials or your name. Now anyone who examines (or admires) your finished pot will know that you made it.

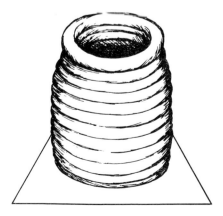

Figure 18.

Set your pot in a safe place in a warm room to dry for about a week. The clay must be completely dry before you can decorate it.

The pot is now ready to be painted. Spread your work area with old newspaper. Place your pot on a small piece of cardboard. This will allow you to turn the pot without touching it.

In painting the Hunny Pot with acrylic or poster paints, you should do the inside of the jar first. You might choose a shade of gold or mustard. Start at the bottom of the jar, then work your way up and around the inside of the jar walls. Be sure to cover the surface completely. When you have finished the inside, paint the outside. Work from the top downward. Allow the pot to dry before you handle it.

Most paints dry in about an hour. For a more durable finish you could seal the pot with a gloss or matt acrylic varnish.

Now that your Hunny Pot is finished, you might use it as a pencil holder or fill it with dried grasses that you have gathered. You might even want to give it to a friend as a useful pot to keep things in.

Caution: Even though your jar has been dried, it is not recommended as a container to hold liquid.

When Eeyore saw the pot, he became quite excited.

"Why!" he said. "I believe my Balloon will just go into that Pot!"

"Oh, no, Eeyore," said Pooh. "Balloons are much too big to go into Pots."

"Not mine," said Eeyore proudly. "Look, Piglet!" And as Piglet looked sorrowfully round, Eeyore picked the balloon up with his teeth, and placed it carefully in the pot; picked it out and put it on the ground; and then picked it up again and put it carefully back.

"So it does!" said Pooh. "It goes in!"

"So it does!" said Piglet. "And it comes out!"

"Doesn't it?" said Eeyore. "It goes in and out like anything."

"I'm very glad," said Pooh happily, "that I thought of giving you a Useful Pot to put things in."   —*Winnie-the-Pooh*

Tiddely-Pom Snow Scene

You will need:
a small, clean plastic jar with watertight lid
light-blue and white enamel model paint
2 small paintbrushes, one with fine tip
a black, waterproof, smearproof, marking pen
a phial of white Christmas glitter
waterproof adhesive, such as epoxy
    or contact cement
a small, china *or* plastic animal that will fit inside

Follow the directions on the adhesive container to fasten the animal (you might want to use a rabbit, as Rabbit has so many relations) to the bottom of the inside of the jar. A baby food jar is excellent to use. Allow the adhesive to dry completely.

While you are waiting for it to dry, paint the jar lid with the light blue model paint, which is available in very small tins. After the paint has dried, use the white paint or the black marker to print, "The more it snows tiddely-pom," on the jar lid. You can add some white dots to represent snowflakes.

When the adhesive and the lid have dried thoroughly, place about two teaspoonsful of the snow glitter in the jar. Next, fill the jar almost to the top with water. The glitter will float, so be careful not to fill the jar too full or it will spill out. Wipe away

any glitter that may be on the mouth of the jar. Replace the lid and screw it on very tightly.

Now your snow scene is finished. To watch it snow inside your jar, shake it, then hold it still, and watch the snow drift around and settle down (Figure 19).

Figure 19.

The more it
SNOWS-tiddely-pom,
The more it
GOES-tiddely-pom
The more it
GOES-tiddely-pom
On
Snowing.
              —*The House at Pooh Corner*